In This Thin Rain

Other Poetry Books By Nelson Ball

Nine Poems (Rubblestone Press, 2011)
Three-Letter Words (Laurel Reed Books, 2006)
At The Edge Of The Frog Pond (The Mercury Press, 2004)
With Held (Laurel Reed Books, 2004)
Scrub Cedar (above/ground press, 2003)
A Gathering (Rubblestone Press, 2003)
Almost Spring (The Mercury Press, 1999)
Visitation (Rubblestone Press, 1998)
To Share That Yellow (fingerprinting inkoperated, 1998)
The Concrete Air (The Mercury Press, 1996)
Round Table (Letters, 1996)
Small Gardens (fingerprinting inkoperated, 1996)
Bird Tracks On Hard Snow (ECW Press, 1994)
Fifteen Poems (MindWare, 1994)
Sightings (Curvd H&z, 1992)
With Issa: Poems 1964-1971 (ECW Press, 1991)
Force Movements (2nd edition, Curvd H&z, 1990)
Round Stone (Weed/Flower Press, 1971)
Points Of Attention (Weed/Flower Press, 1971)
The Pre-Linguistic Heights (Coach House Press, 1970)
Water-Pipes And Moonlight (Weed/Flower Press, 1969)
Force Movements (Ganglia Press, 1969)
Sparrows (Weed/Flower Press, 1968)
Beaufort's Scale (Weed/Flower Press, 1967)
Room Of Clocks (Weed/Flower Press, 1965)

Books Edited

Konfessions Of An Elizabethan Fan Dancer by bpNichol (Coach House Books, 2004)
Frank Harrington's Kristmiss Book (The Mercury Press, 1993)

In This Thin Rain

Nelson Ball

Mansfield Press

a stuart ross book

Printed in Canada

Library and Archives Canada Cataloguing in Publication

Ball, Nelson, 1942-
In this thin rain / Nelson Ball.

Poems.
ISBN 978-1-894469-66-1

I. Title.

PS8503.A59I53 2012 C811'.54 C2012-900850-8

Editor for the press: Stuart Ross
Cover design: Denis De Klerck
Cover image: iStockphoto
Typesetting: Stuart Ross
Author photo: Patrick Campbell

The publication of *In This Thin Rain* has been generously supported by the Canada Council for the Arts and the Ontario Arts Council.

Canada Council for the Arts Conseil des Arts du Canada
ONTARIO ARTS COUNCIL CONSEIL DES ARTS DE L'ONTARIO

Mansfield Press Inc.
25 Mansfield Avenue, Toronto, Ontario, Canada M6J 2A9
Publisher: Denis De Klerck
www.mansfieldpress.net

In memory of Barbara Caruso

Contents

Geese

Honking
geese

speak

their
speech

honk

or
squawk

their
talk

Together

In the low breeze
two trees squeak

Along The Nith River

steep banks
ten feet high along the ancient valley floor

host a chaos
of plant growth

eroded by fast water cutting
into soil and gravel

unrooting
shrubs

felling
trees

Ducks

Ducks
are everywhere

this
wet spring

I saw one
swimming

in a roadside
puddle

Communications Tower On Green Lane

Honking
geese

fly
by

the tall
silent

steel
structure

At The Farmer's Dell Plaza, Brantford

lighting fixtures
        removed
                along the soffit

leave holes
        large enough
                for sparrows

to squeeze through
        nesting
                thriving

the sole wildlife
        visible
                in this paved land

Anti-Gothic

Shaped
by earliest morning light

from night's
opaque blackness

into looming
dark masses —

trees, cars
buildings —

the things
of this world

Centipede At Midnight

startled
it fell

off
the wall

startling
me

Cobweb

Across the back window
a large cobweb

almost
invisible

holds
suspended

grass
and twigs

dropped
by nest-building birds

from
the soffit high above

Relativity

One end
of a very long train

is leaving Paris
while the other end

hasn't
arrived

Dead Flies

I

Three small piles
          of grey dust

flies expired
          on white paper —

a sheet for notes
          easily brushed off

II (with boots on)

Resting
on hind legs and rearmost tips

of
wings

          tilted
          like a rocket launcher

it died
just like that

Anticipation

Wind
rattles leaves

a sound
like rainfall

soon
to strike

How Low

the birds fly
across this wooded county road

a foot
above ground

in front
of the car

All Day

sky
dull

darker
now

wind
rising, every

leaf
moving

rain
near

soon

After The Rain

After last night's wind-driven rain
the Nith is wide and muddy

on its surface flecks of foam
break and mingle forming new shapes

the brown water
has a greenish cast

reflecting light from the shorelines'
luxuriant growth

swallows slip through the air
just below the bridge

or fuss
at the riverbank

Fly

On a sunny morning by the creek
a fly buzzes around my head

it intermittently
breaks the silence

is this the sound
of morning light?

Leaf

A single leaf caught
in a long narrow breeze

dances, runs
on the spot

not going
anywhere

Electricity Arrives At The Cottage

Above
dense green bush

emerges
shiny and new

a hydro pole
wires attached

Summer 2008

for Patrick Campbell who found the leak & repaired it

Spring
and summer

too
much
rain

too
heavy

too
often

leaking
into

our
wall

On The Rail Trail

Damselflies
hover and shift near the ground

visible only
in sunlit patches

A Crow

at the roadside
is busy turning

a dead chipmunk
into crow

Obituaries

Lately
I've been reading obituaries

don't quite
know why

lives are
always ending

always

Reprieve

I thought that rooves
was the plural of roof

like hoof
and hooves

aloud, I still say rooves
not roofs

dogs roof
rooves is not in my dictionaries

but aha
it appears in poems

by Basil Bunting
and William Carlos Williams

Anomaly

Water
        air and light —

the tentative materiality
        of clouds

        so sharply
delineated

Idleness

On this hot day
I feel languid

watching
the south wind

bend
grasses

toward an
oncoming storm

The Old House

seems
propped up

by a newly painted down pipe
standing at one corner

Checkmate

> *News item: "Oxford dictionary drops the dash" by Simon Rabinovitch, as it appeared in* The Globe and Mail, *Sept. 24, 2007*

About 16,000 words have
  succumbed to pressures
  of the Internet age and
lost their hyphens in a new
edition of the *Shorter Oxford*
English Dictionary.
  Bumble-bee is now bumble-
bee. . . .
  And if you've got a problem
with that, don't be such a cry-
baby (formerly cry-baby).
  The hyphen has been
squeezed as informal ways of
communicating . . . seep into
newspapers and books. . . .

Heron

With remarkably laboured
flapping of wings

the great blue heron
moves slowly above

Highway 401's
fast moving traffic

In The Wind

Voluminous trees
grow larger in shape

by their leaves'
continuous agitation

**

Long rows of spruce sway
while the jack pine

loosens iconic form
to surprised motion

Anomaly

In the bean field
corn stalks
stalk
beans

Question

Grey
on grey

a tall dead tree
in the distance

is it behind
or in front of

that
barn?

Anomaly

Cement
angels

Storm Warning

Wavering grasses
bend northward

clouds go dark
rolling, turning

mixing, motion
without rest

generating
dark colours

July

brings
blues —

skirting
roadsides —

chicory
and blue devil

Crickets

Crickets climb
the foundation of our house

then fall or jump off
or climb down

to what purpose
all this climbing, I ask

then realize
why not

Evocation

Virtually perfect
parallel rows of corn stubble

remind me
of Barbara's drawings

Colours

thinking of Barbara

Yellows and browns —
a field of beans ripening in September

sunlight now
more yellow than white

coloured light, reflecting rich ochres
of the field of beans

this day
in September

An October Day At The Mount Pleasant Ponds, Mourning

Brown
pine needles

float
on water

among a few leaves
and twigs

**

I look for fish
see none, but

water striders
in action

cast
indistinct shadows

on pond
bottom

**

Some
days

I startle
at my shadow

**

A soft
thud

on my hat
nothing more

than
a falling leaf

**

Leaves
fall slowly today

I
count them

birds
seem undisturbed

by
my presence

Still

A
crow

hangs
in the air

facing
the strong wind

still
there

Night Wind Indicator

Outside
my window

tips
of the yew's branches

rasp
across the screen

back
and forth

fingering
consciousness

The Windmill

There are no signs
in this large field of corn stubble

of the house and barn taken down
to enlarge the field, except

standing
abandoned

at the roadside
a conked-out windmill

Walking

Early
October, mild

walking
at The Ponds

sunny
no clouds

breeze
enough to make

trees
restless

as
I am

some
leaves

are
falling

Persistence

This decrepit windmill
still faces west

Semblance

The spruce's branches
agitated in high wind

resemble
the lake's

choppy
surface

An

otter
oughtn’t

swim
in

choppy
water

November

Tamarack needles
along the road's shoulder

muted
yellow ochre

gold
in this thin rain

What Remain

What remain
of the dead tree's branches

wiggle
in the stiff wind

Late Fall

I

A circular pool
yellow ochre
beneath the small maple

II

A yellow maple leaf
caught on
the yew's green branch

III

Massive grey clouds
constrict
sunset's blush

Bucolic

When the leaves have fallen
this rural landscape reveals

abandoned farmhouses
worn-out cars and trucks

rusted farm machinery
collapsed sheds and barns

Ider Oads Or Side Winder

roadside
oadsider
adsidero
dsideroa
sideroad
ideroads
deroadsi
eroadsid
roadside

Drumbeat For Drumbo

Drumbo is a village in southwestern Ontario
(Composed by the Microsoft Word 2003 spell-checker)

Dumb
Drub
Rumba
Rambo
Drubs
Drum
Drumbeat
Drum Bo
Crumb

Old News

News item, CTV.ca News Staff, Feb. 4, 2009

"Ancient . . . snakes
ate crocs for breakfast"

news of snakes
fifty feet long

sixty million
years ago

reaches
today

On The Rail Trail

The shadow of a turkey vulture
flits from tree trunk to tree trunk

Pines

In the deciduous bush
browns and greys

then
pale greens

of surprising
pines

December

drowsy
        housefly
                walks

A Walk In The Snow

When the heart breaks
snowflakes

on the face
hide tears

Large Maple In Winter

Thousands of twigs
and twiglets

charged
by the wind

black filigree
in subtle dances

against
grey sky

Farm Market Reports

An abandoned windmill
sits atop a thirty-foot four-legged tower

wires dangle
from the disabled generator

blades missing
from the seized-up propeller

long ago it brought
words through the air

by charging a battery
that powered a radio

brought news
to the farmer milking cows by lantern light

farm market reports
to the wood stove heated farmhouse

hidden in summer
by roadside trees and shrubs

now clearly
visible

this cold
winter morning

Midwinter Thaw

On the lawn
        dog poop near
                a red cardinal

A Soft Day

A day
in mid-February

temperature rising
from zero to ten

the air
visible

a soft day
my grandmother

would
say

a grey
day

On The River

when sheet ice cracks
the sound explodes

muffled, like
the distant

discharge
of a shotgun

A Fallen Tree

roots
upturned

trunk
embedded in river's ice

bark
eroded

awaits
release

into spring's
fast water

January Fly

I watch
a drowsy January fly

try
to walk up the baseboard

reaching
two inches of height

before falling
on its back, then

slowly
right itself

and
to my astonishment

try
to fly

reaching
an elevation of maybe three inches

and a lesser
distance forward

then
drop

to the floor
exhausted —

difficult
days

Snowdrifts

Snow crowds
around

the abandoned
farmhouse

waiting
to be let in

In A Barren Tree In Winter

Birds

appear

like

old

leaves

Bannister Lake

Bannister Lake
is missing

in the vast
expanse

of
snow

On The Grand River

February
thaw

small
pieces of ice

bits
of wood

rush
by

large
ice slabs

lodge
among

shoreline
trees

Notes And Acknowledgements

This book is dedicated to the memory of Barbara Caruso, my wife and soulmate, who died in December 2009. Barbara was a brilliant visual artist, a skilled writer and an enriching companion. We were together for 44 years. She taught me to see, and especially, to see colour.

My mother, Frances (Mossop) Ball, was a bird watcher, plant collector and guardian of nature. She taught by her example respect for, and recognition of, the autonomy of the natural world. She died in April 2011.

I am grateful to these two singular people. They enlarged my life enormously. I miss them both.

Barbara read drafts of poems in this book written in 2009. They benefited from her comments and suggestions.

Since writing the poem "Reprieve", I've found "rooves" as an alternative plural of "roof" in two large dictionaries and one shorter one. It appears in the *Shorter Oxford English Dictionary* (6th edition, 2007) and *Webster's Third New International Dictionary* (updated to 2002), and, oddly, in the *Gage Canadian Dictionary* (1983). "Rooves" doesn't appear in *The Compact Edition of the Oxford English Dictionary* [microprint] (1971) nor in the *Canadian Oxford Dictionary* (2nd edition, 2004) nor the *Concise Oxford English Dictionary* (11th edition, revised, 2006). *The Oxford Guide to Canadian English Usage* (2nd edition, 2007) by Margery Fee and Janice McAlpine gives "roofs" as the accepted plural. *Merriam-Webster's Collegiate Dictionary* (11th edition, 2007) gives only "roofs". It's interesting that concise dictionaries are created by omitting not only main entries, but also variant plurals. My survey was informal and far from complete.

Thank you to Stuart Ross for his friendship and for his astute editing of this book. Stuart made a preliminary selection of poems when I couldn't get started. Stuart and Kemeny Babineau each read the poems and made helpful suggestions for revision. Thanks to Denis De Klerck for the cover design and for publishing this book.

Thanks to Kemeny, Liz Ball, Patrick Campbell, Brian David Johnston, Patricia Moore, Jackie Morris and Mary Neff for ruminative talks and walks and friendship.

I am grateful to Bob Tees, Sheila Vollmer, Katie Webb and Jill Yuzwa who each brought light to a difficult time.

"Drumbeat For Drumbo" was published as a leaflet by Laurel Reed Books in 2010.

Some of the poems have been published in *Hardscrabble, The New Chief Tongue, This Magazine, 1cent* and *Tract.*

Thanks to the editors of those publications: M.R. Appell, Kemeny Babineau, jwcurry and Stuart Ross.

The poems in this book were written from 2009 to 2011 with the exception of "Bannister Lake", written in 2002.

Nelson Ball
January 2012

Nelson Ball is a poet and bookseller living in Paris, Ontario. He has worked as a labourer, chauffeur, clerk, seasonal forest ranger, record store clerk and janitor. From 1965 to 1973 he ran the legendary Weed/Flower Press, publishing mimeo editions of early books by Victor Coleman, Carol Bergé, David McFadden, bill bissett, bpNichol and many others. He is the author of 25 poetry books and chapbooks.

Other Books From Mansfield Press

Poetry

Stephen Brockwell & Stuart Ross, eds., *Rogue Stimulus: The Stephen Harper Holiday Anthology for a Prorogued Parliament*
Alice Burdick, *Holler*
Gary Michael Dault, *The Milk of Birds*
Pier Giorgio Di Cicco, *Early Works*
Christopher Doda, *Aesthetics Lesson*
Rishma Dunlop, *Lover Through Departure: New and Selected Poems*
Jaime Forsythe, *Sympathy Loophole*
Jason Heroux, *Emergency Hallelujah*
David W. McFadden, *What's the Score?*
Leigh Nash, *Goodbye, Ukulele*
Lillian Necakov, *Hooligans*
Peter Norman, *At the Gates of the Theme Park*
Natasha Nuhanovic, *Stray Dog Embassy*
Catherine Owen & Joe Rosenblatt, with Karen Moe, *Dog*
Jim Smith, *Back Off, Assassin! New & Selected Poems*
Robert Earl Stewart, *Campfire Radio Rhapsody*
Carey Toane, *The Crystal Palace*
Priscila Uppal, *Winter Sport: Poems*
Steve Venright, *Floors of Enduring Beauty*

Fiction

Marianne Apostolides, *The Lucky Child*
Kent Nussey, *A Love Supreme*
Marko Sijan, *Mongrel*
Tom Walmsley, *Dog Eat Rat*

Non-Fiction

George Bowering, *How I Wrote Certain of My Books*
Pier Giorgio Di Cicco, *Municipal Mind*
Amy Lavender Harris, *Imagining Toronto*

For a complete list of Mansfield Press titles, please visit mansfieldpress.net